Stamp Album

This album belongs to

Stamp Album

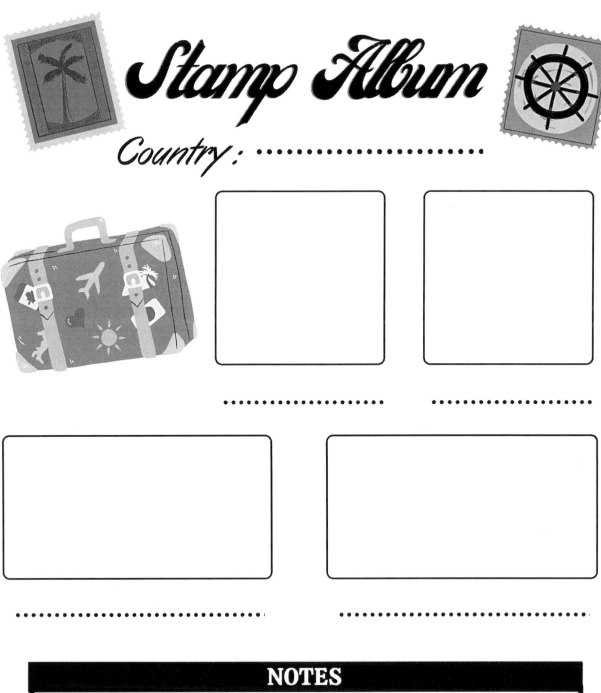

Country: ....

NOTES

....
....
....
....
....

Stamp Album

Country: ....

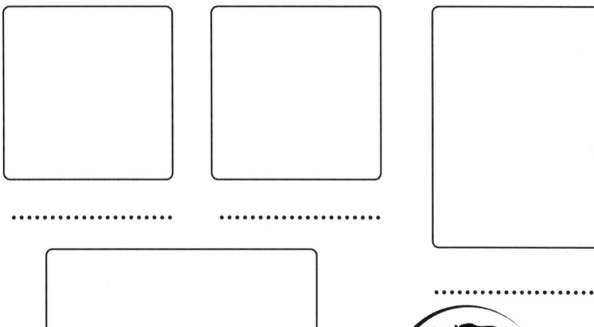

....

....

....

NOTES

....

....

....

....

....

Stamp Album

Country: ....

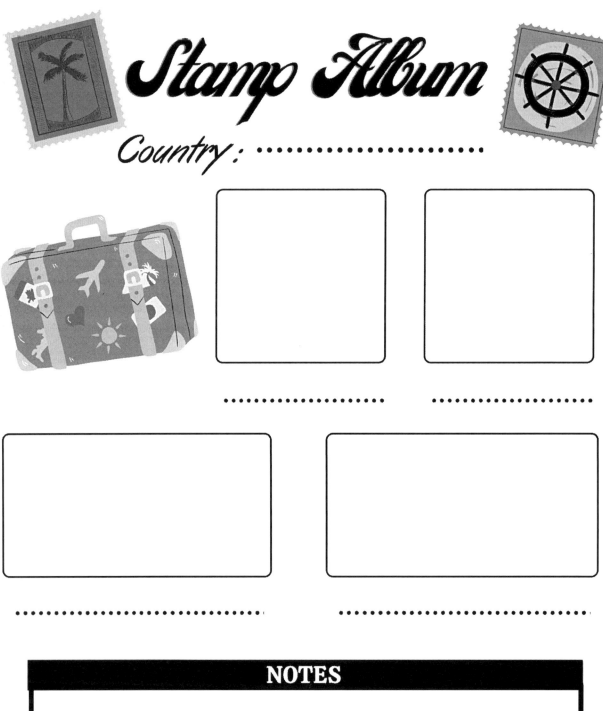

....

....

NOTES

Stamp Album

Country: ....

....

....

....

NOTES

....

....

....

....

....

Stamp Album

Country: ∙∙∙∙∙∙∙∙∙∙∙∙∙∙∙∙∙∙∙∙∙

∙∙∙∙∙∙∙∙∙∙∙∙∙∙∙∙∙∙∙∙∙∙∙∙∙∙ ∙∙∙∙∙∙∙∙∙∙∙∙∙∙∙∙∙∙∙∙∙∙∙∙∙∙

∙∙∙∙∙∙∙∙∙∙∙∙∙∙∙∙∙∙∙∙∙∙∙∙∙∙ ∙∙∙∙∙∙∙∙∙∙∙∙∙∙∙∙∙∙∙∙∙∙∙∙∙∙

NOTES

Stamp Album

Country: ....

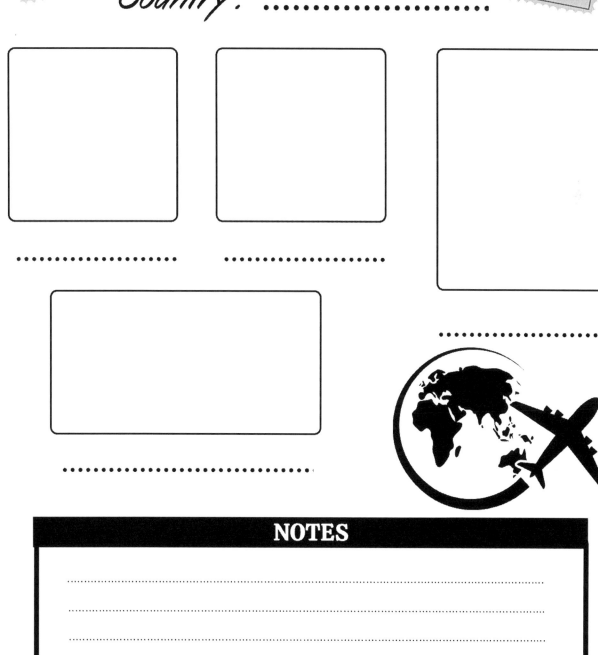

NOTES

....
....
....
....
....

Stamp Album

Country: ....

....

....

NOTES

....

....

....

....

....

Stamp Album

Country: ....

....

....

....

....

NOTES

....

....

....

....

....

Stamp Album

Country : ....

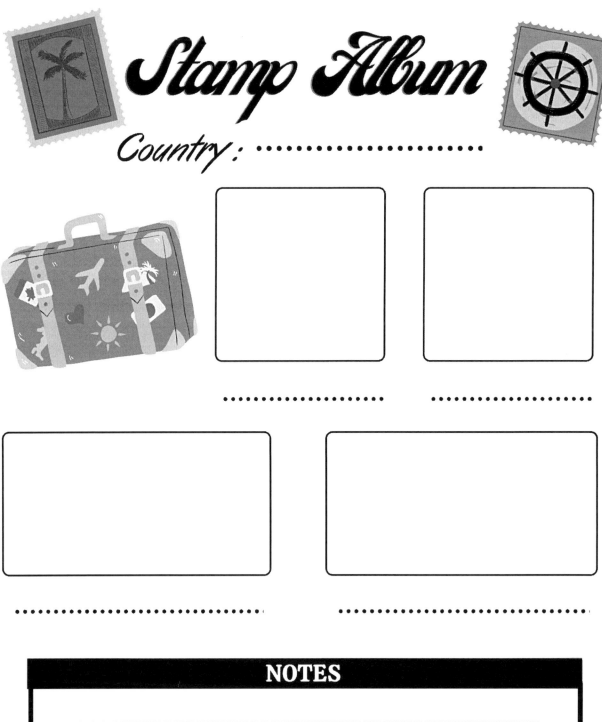

....

....

NOTES

....
....
....
....
....

Stamp Album

Country: ....

....

....

....

....

NOTES

....

....

....

....

....

Stamp Album

Country: ....

....

....

NOTES

....
....
....
....
....

Stamp Album

Country: ....

....

....

....

NOTES

....

....

....

....

....

Stamp Album

Country: ....

....

....

NOTES

....

....

....

....

....

Stamp Album

Country: ....

NOTES

Stamp Album

Country: ....

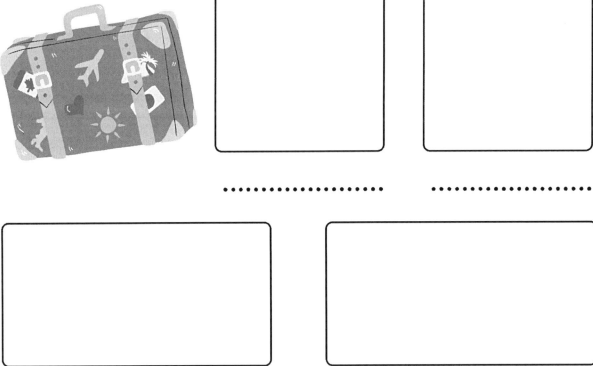

....

....

NOTES

....

....

....

....

....

Stamp Album

Country: ....

....

....

....

NOTES

Stamp Album

Country : ....

NOTES

....

....

....

....

....

Stamp Album

Country: ....

NOTES
....
....
....
....
....

Stamp Album

Country: ....

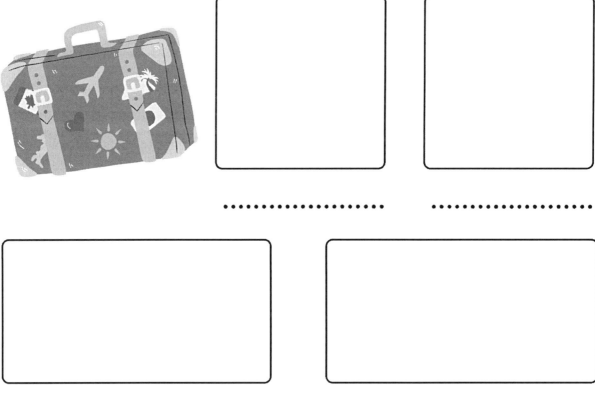

NOTES

....

....

....

....

....

Stamp Album

Country: ....

NOTES

Stamp Album

Country : ....

....

....

NOTES

....

....

....

....

....

Stamp Album

Country: ....

....

....

....

NOTES

....

....

....

....

....

Stamp Album

Country: ....

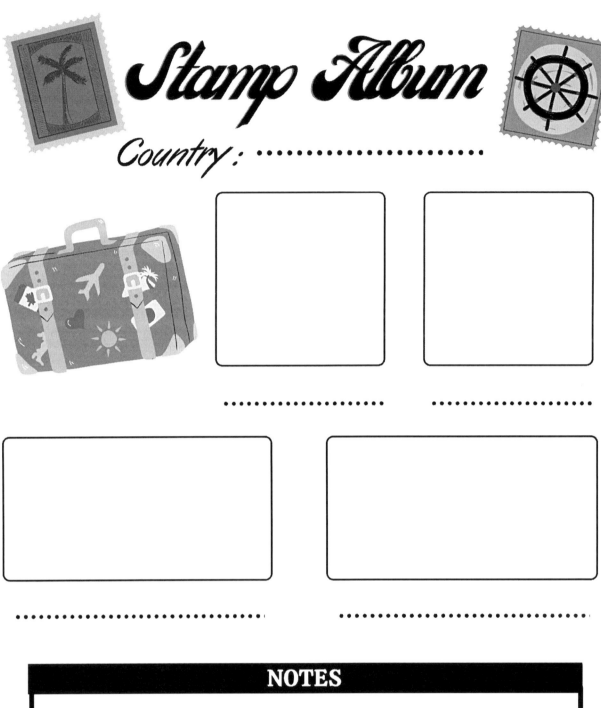

....

....

NOTES

....

....

....

....

....

Stamp Album

Country: ....

....

....

....

....

NOTES

Stamp Album

Country: ....

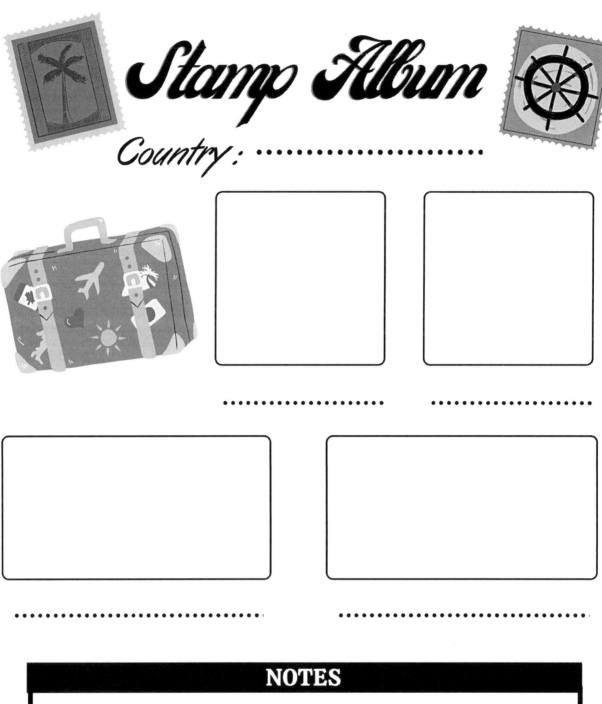

....

....

NOTES

....

....

....

....

....

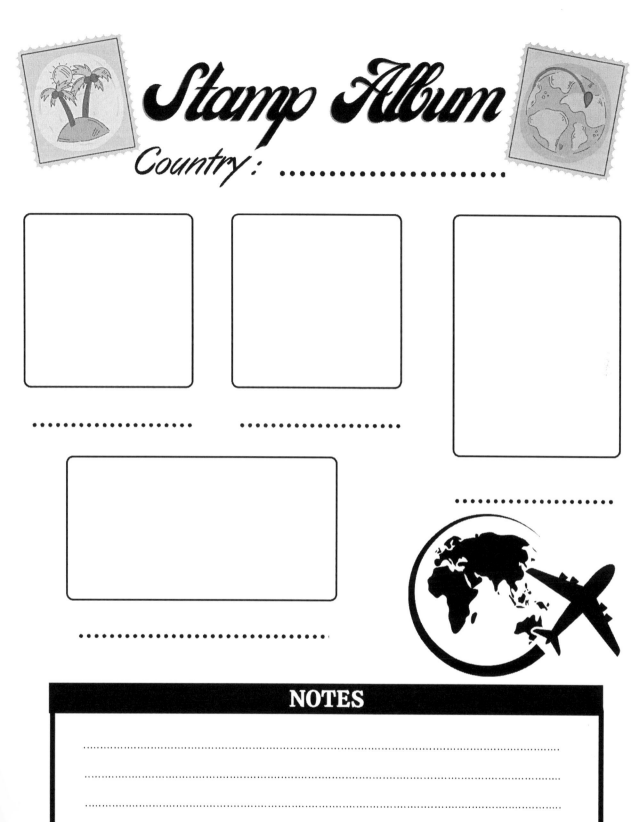

Stamp Album

Country: ....

NOTES

....

....

....

....

....

Stamp Album

Country: ....

NOTES

....

....

....

....

....

Stamp Album

Country: ....

....

....

....

....

NOTES

....

....

....

....

....

Stamp Album

Country: ....

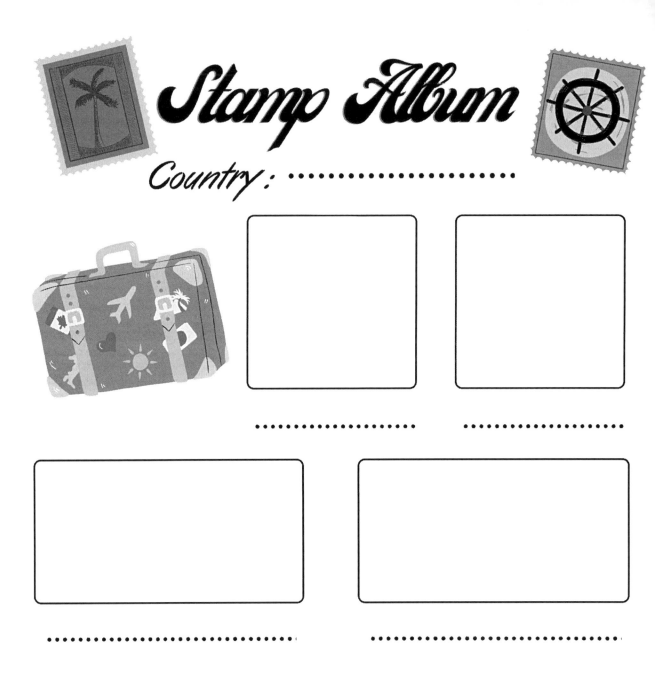

NOTES

....

....

....

....

....

Stamp Album

Country: ....

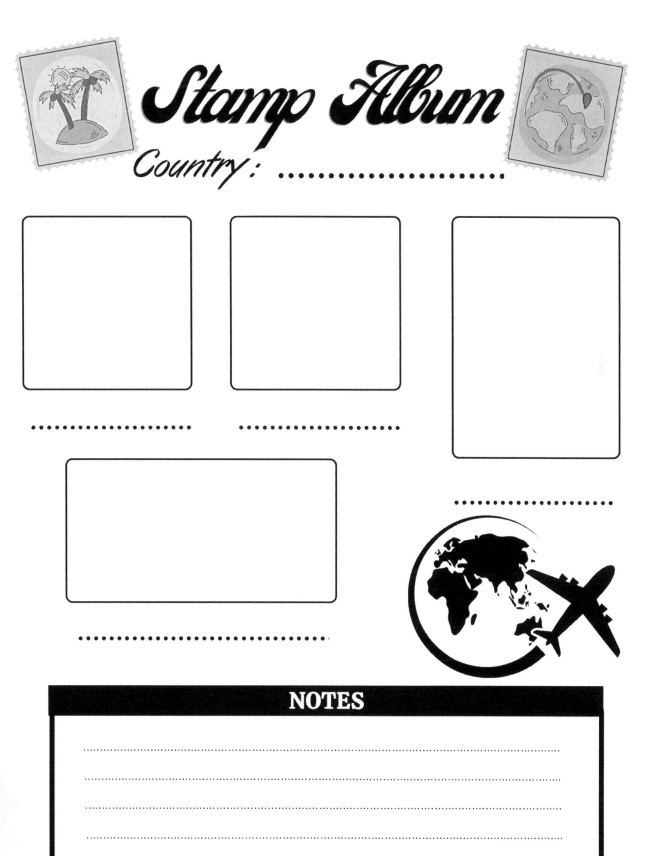

....

....

....

NOTES

....

....

....

....

....

Stamp Album

Country: ....

NOTES

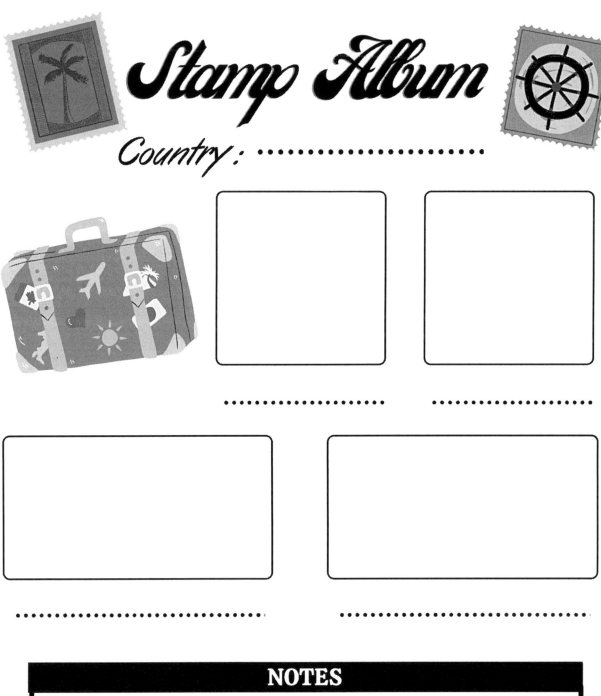

Stamp Album

Country: ....

....

....

....

....

NOTES

Stamp Album

Country: ....

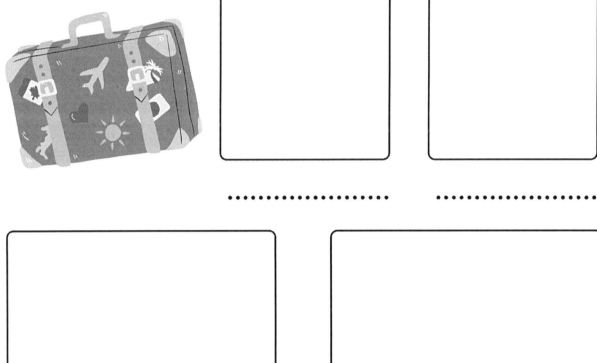

NOTES

....
....
....
....
....

Stamp Album

Country: ....

....

....

....

NOTES

Stamp Album

Country: ⋯⋯⋯⋯⋯⋯⋯⋯⋯

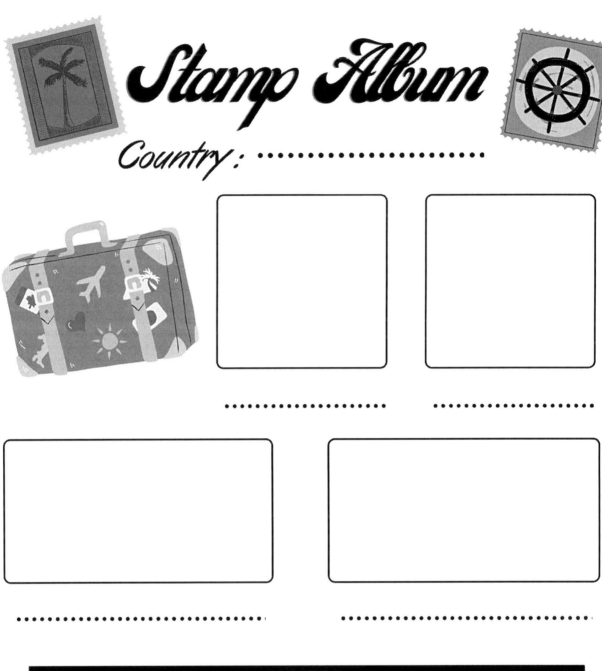

⋯⋯⋯⋯⋯⋯⋯⋯   ⋯⋯⋯⋯⋯⋯⋯⋯

⋯⋯⋯⋯⋯⋯⋯⋯   ⋯⋯⋯⋯⋯⋯⋯⋯

NOTES

⋯⋯⋯⋯⋯⋯⋯⋯⋯⋯⋯⋯⋯⋯⋯⋯⋯⋯⋯⋯⋯⋯⋯⋯⋯⋯⋯

⋯⋯⋯⋯⋯⋯⋯⋯⋯⋯⋯⋯⋯⋯⋯⋯⋯⋯⋯⋯⋯⋯⋯⋯⋯⋯⋯

⋯⋯⋯⋯⋯⋯⋯⋯⋯⋯⋯⋯⋯⋯⋯⋯⋯⋯⋯⋯⋯⋯⋯⋯⋯⋯⋯

⋯⋯⋯⋯⋯⋯⋯⋯⋯⋯⋯⋯⋯⋯⋯⋯⋯⋯⋯⋯⋯⋯⋯⋯⋯⋯⋯

⋯⋯⋯⋯⋯⋯⋯⋯⋯⋯⋯⋯⋯⋯⋯⋯⋯⋯⋯⋯⋯⋯⋯⋯⋯⋯⋯

Stamp Album

Country: ....

NOTES

Stamp Album

Country: ....

NOTES

Stamp Album

Country: ....

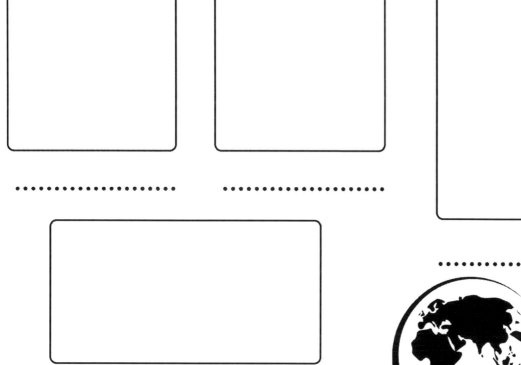

....

....

....

....

NOTES

....

....

....

....

....

Stamp Album

Country: ....

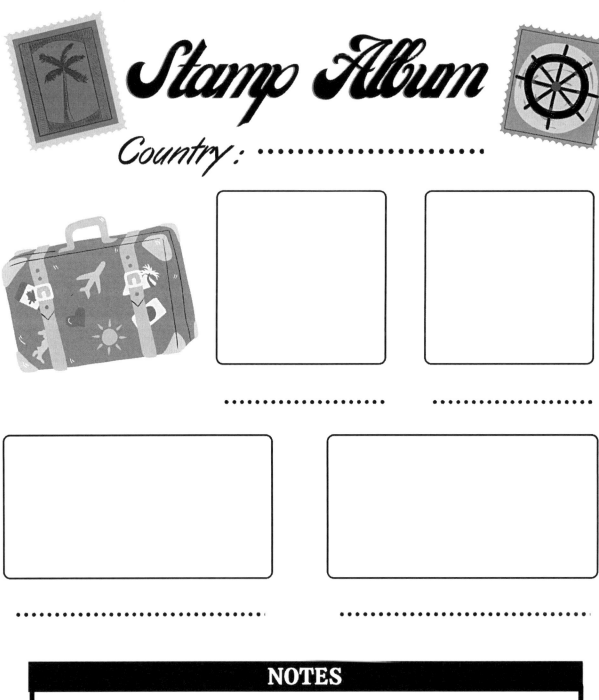

....

....

NOTES

....

....

....

....

....

Stamp Album

Country: ....

NOTES

Stamp Album

Country: ....

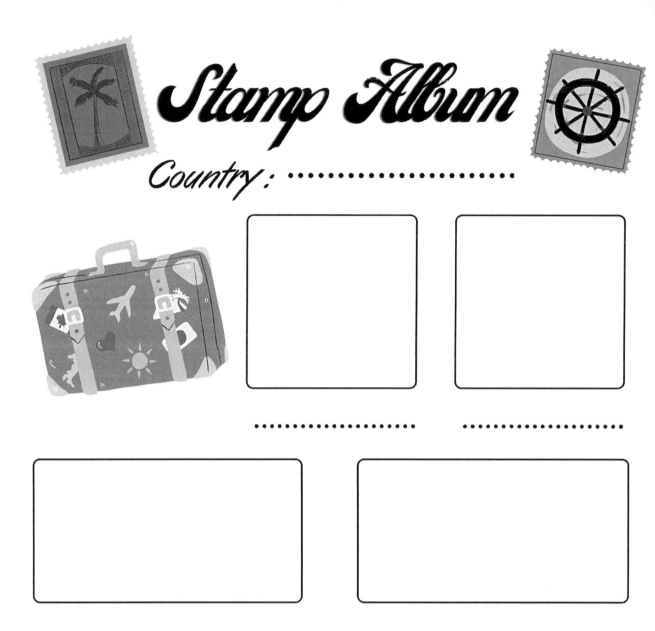

NOTES

....

....

....

....

....

Stamp Album

Country: ....

....

....

....

NOTES

....

....

....

....

....

Stamp Album

Country: ....

....

....

NOTES

....
....
....
....
....

Stamp Album

Country: ....

....

....

....

NOTES

....
....
....
....
....

Stamp Album

Country: ....

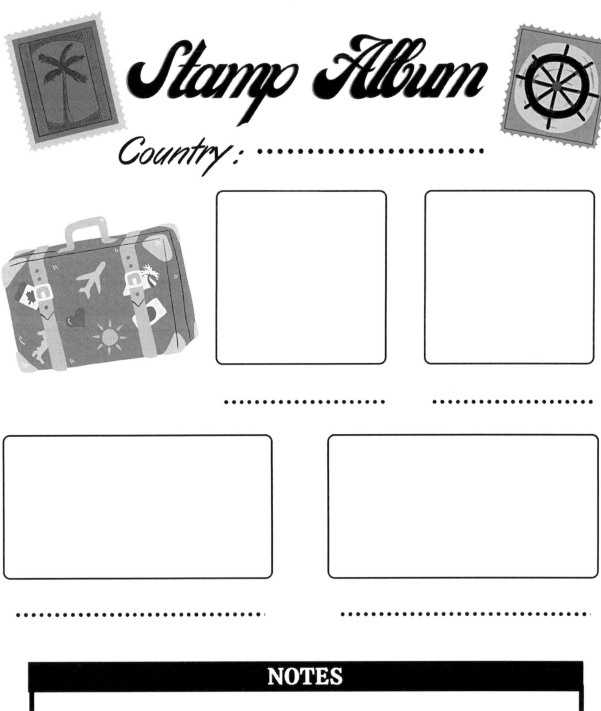

....

....

NOTES

....

....

....

....

....

Stamp Album

Country: ....

NOTES

Stamp Album

Country: ....

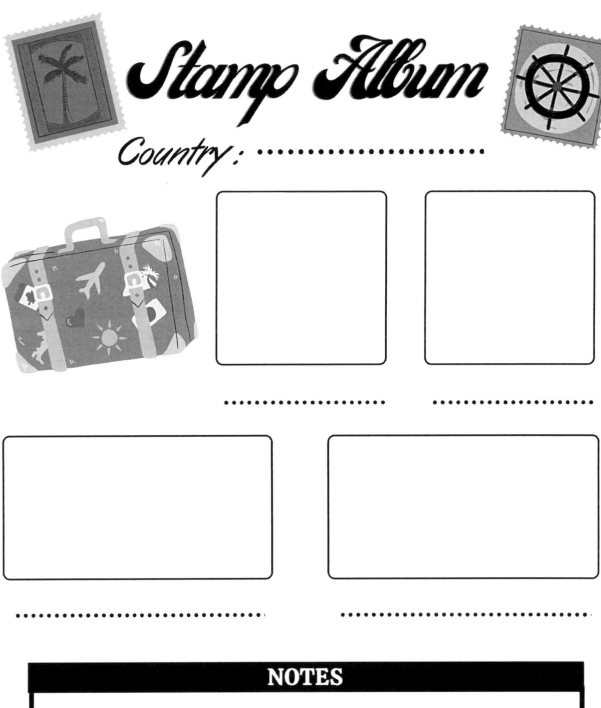

....

....

NOTES

....

....

....

....

....

Stamp Album

Country: ....

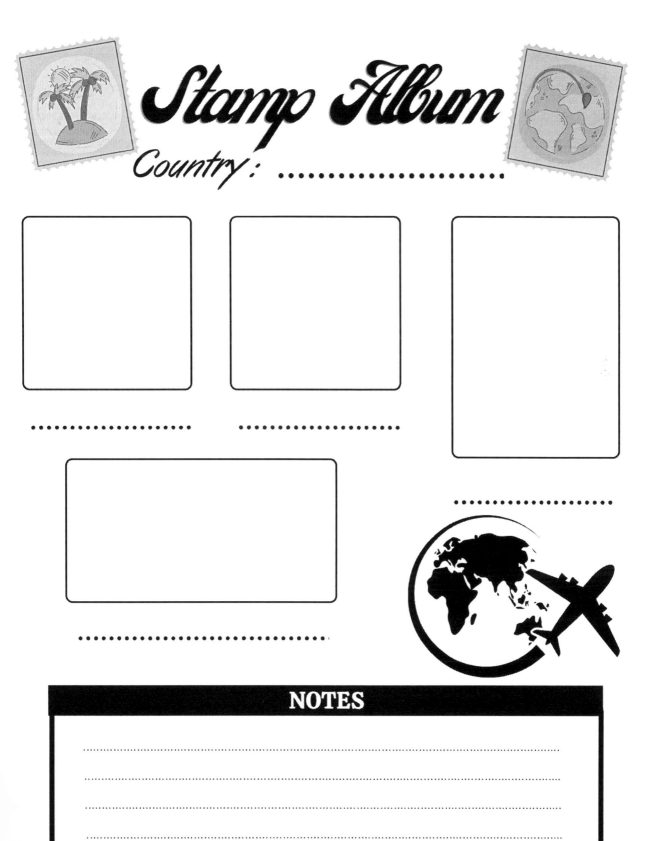

....

....

....

....

NOTES

Stamp Album

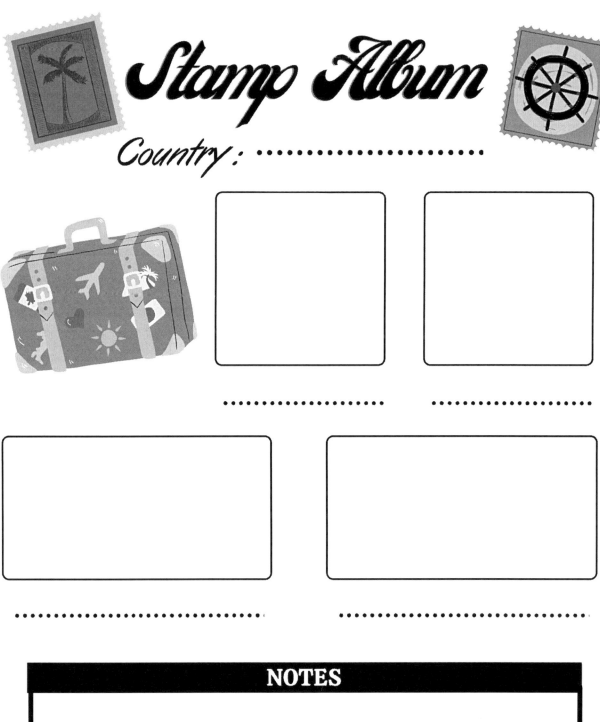

Country: ·······················

NOTES

···
···
···
···
···

Stamp Album

Country: ....

NOTES

....

....

....

....

....

Stamp Album

Country : ....

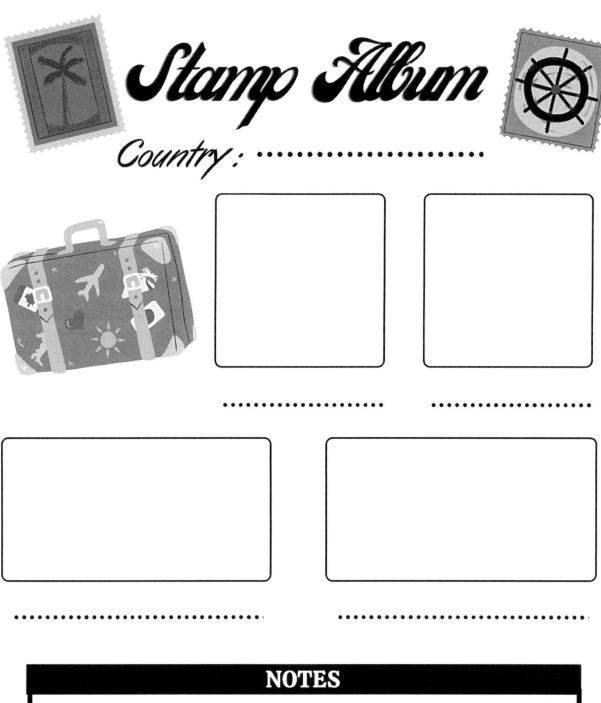

....

....

NOTES

Stamp Album

Country: ....

NOTES

Stamp Album

Country: ....

NOTES

....
....
....
....
....

Stamp Album

Country: ....

NOTES

Stamp Album

Country: ....

....

....

NOTES

....
....
....
....
....

Stamp Album

Country: ....

....
....

....

....

NOTES

....
....
....
....
....

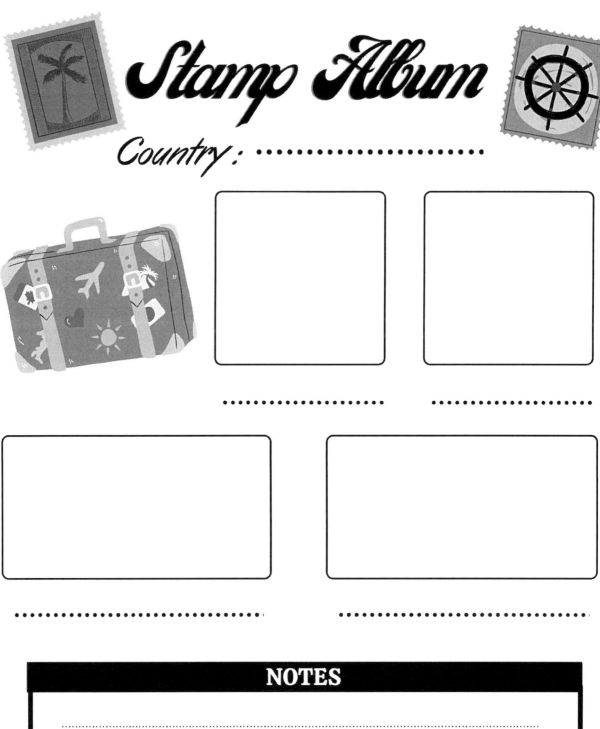

Stamp Album

Country: ....

NOTES

Stamp Album

Country: ....

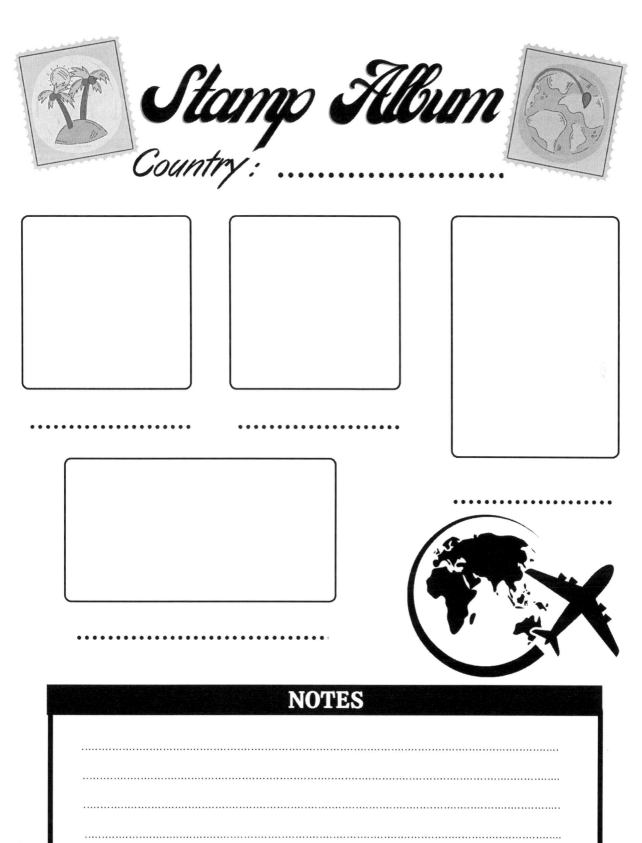

NOTES

Stamp Album

Country: ⋯⋯⋯⋯⋯⋯⋯⋯

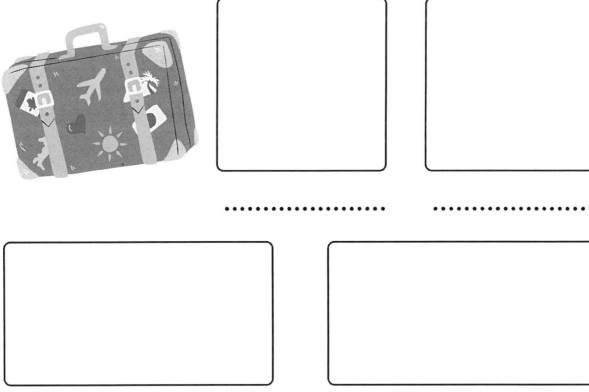

⋯⋯⋯⋯⋯⋯⋯⋯   ⋯⋯⋯⋯⋯⋯⋯⋯

⋯⋯⋯⋯⋯⋯⋯⋯   ⋯⋯⋯⋯⋯⋯⋯⋯

NOTES

Stamp Album

Country: ....

NOTES

Stamp Album

Country: ....

NOTES

....
....
....
....
....

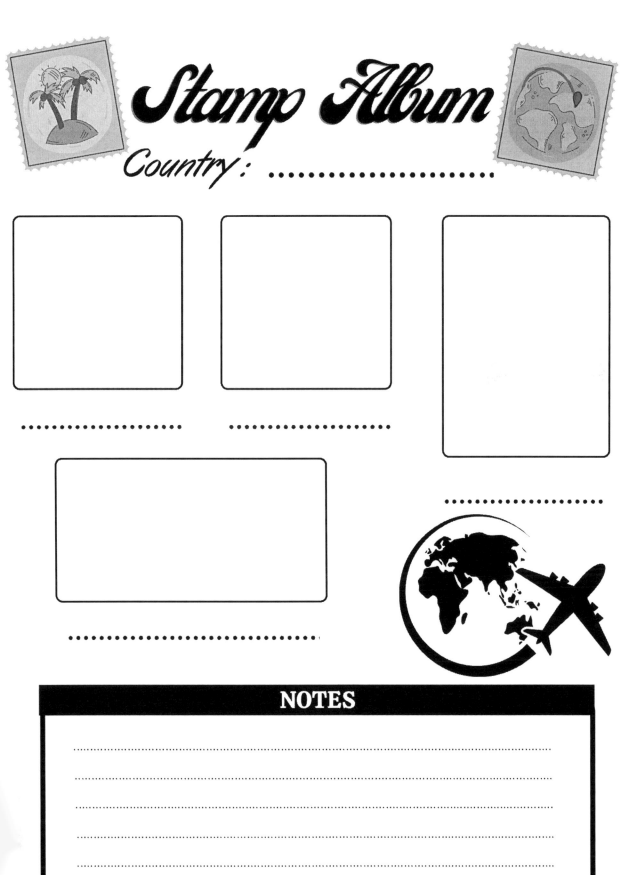

Stamp Album

Country: ....

NOTES

Stamp Album

Country: ....

NOTES

....

....

....

....

....

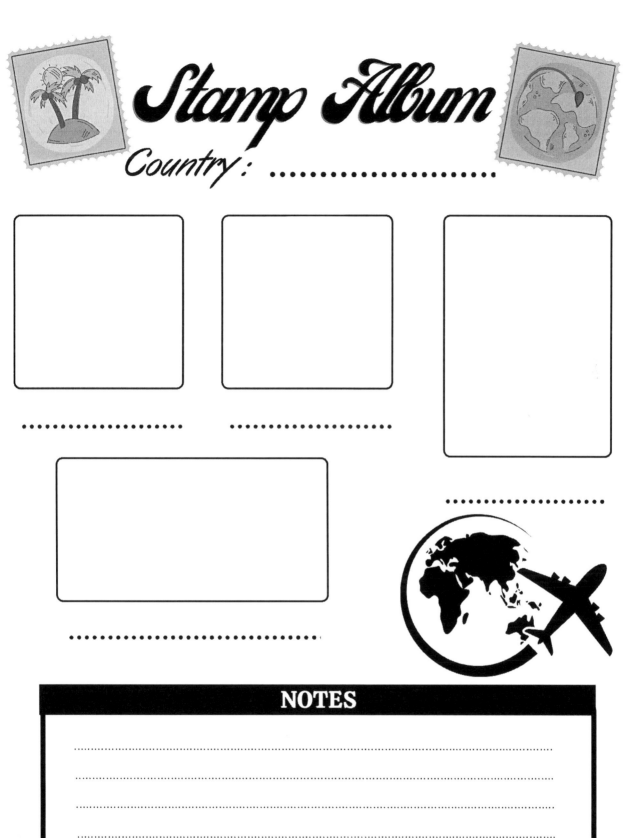

Stamp Album

Country: ....

NOTES

Stamp Album

Country: ....

....

....

NOTES

....

....

....

....

....

Stamp Album

Country: ....

NOTES
....
....
....
....
....

Stamp Album

Country: ⋯⋯⋯⋯⋯⋯

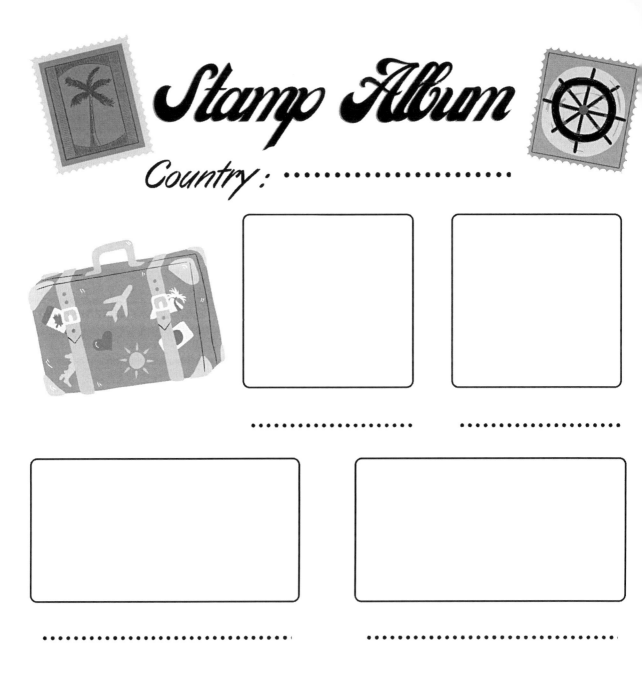

NOTES

Stamp Album

Country: ....

NOTES

Stamp Album

Country: ....

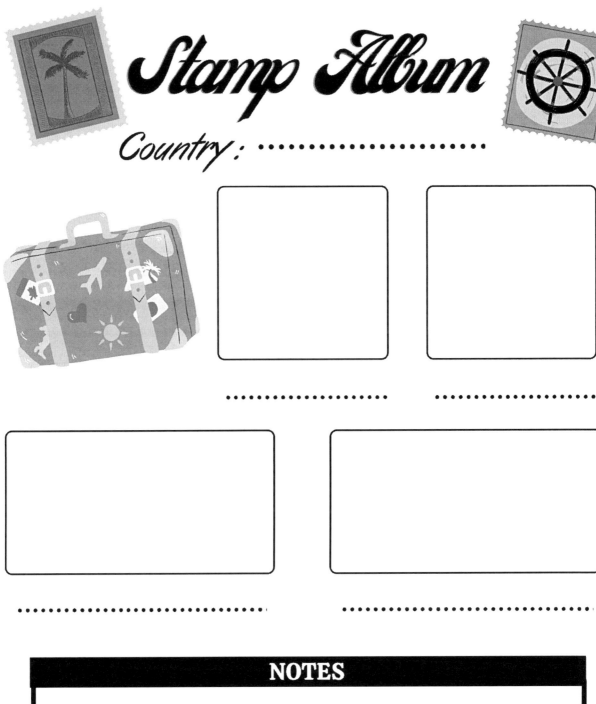

....

....

NOTES

....

....

....

....

....

Stamp Album

Country: ....

NOTES

Stamp Album

Country: ....

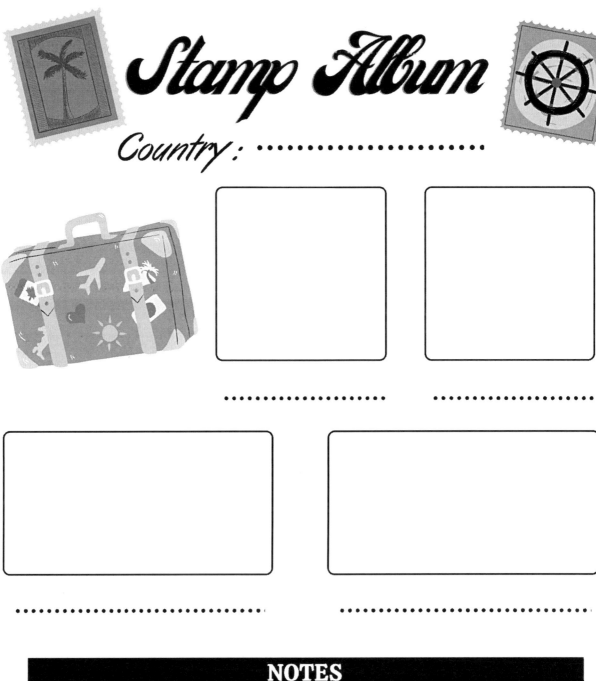

....

....

NOTES

....
....
....
....
....

Stamp Album

Country: ....

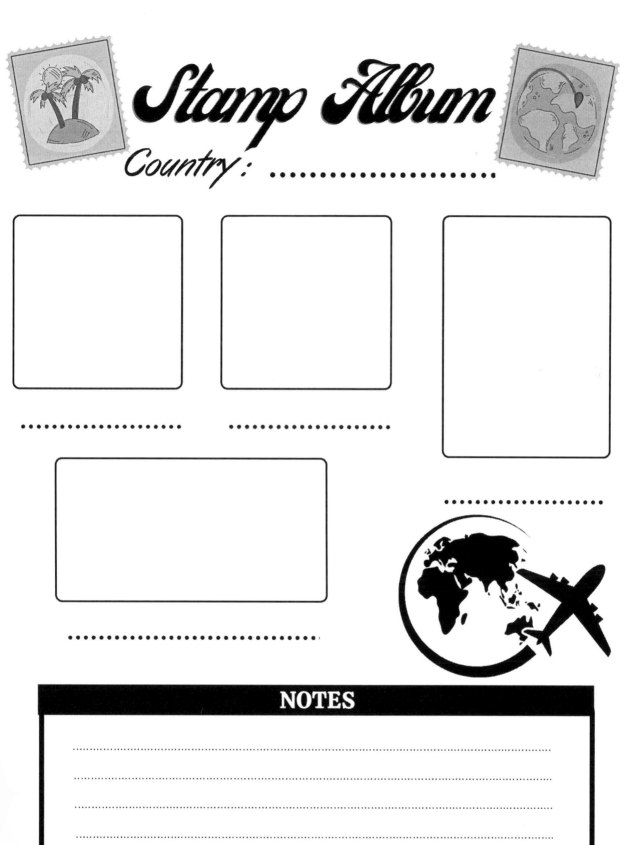

NOTES

Stamp Album

Country: ....

....

....

NOTES

....

....

....

....

....

Stamp Album

Country: ....

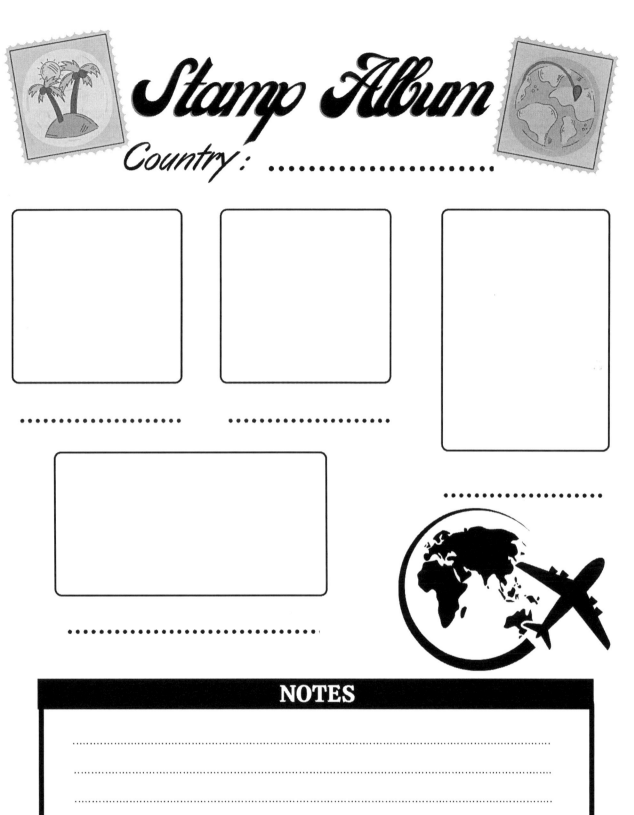

....

....

....

NOTES

....

....

....

....

....

Stamp Album

Country: ....

NOTES

....

....

....

....

....

Stamp Album

Country: ....

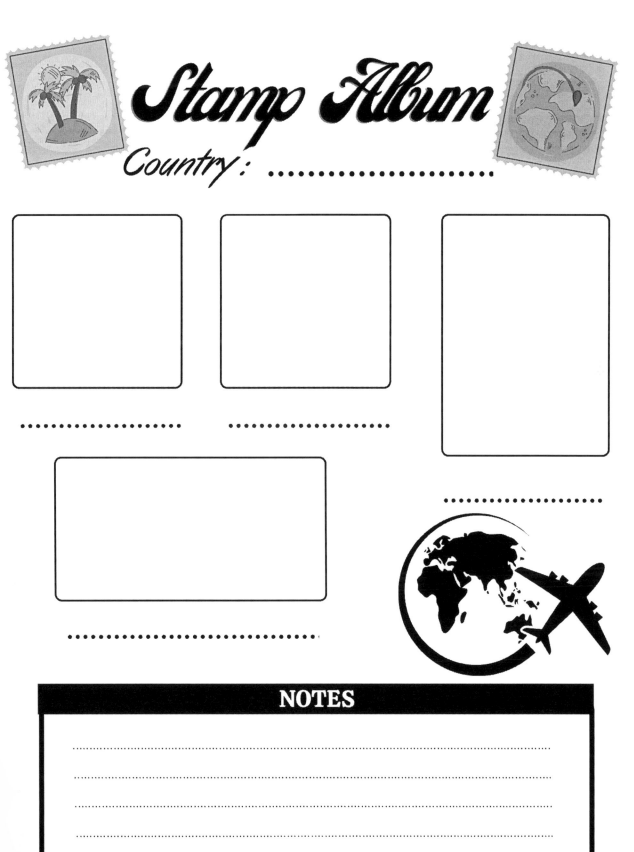

....

....

....

....

NOTES

Stamp Album

Country: ....

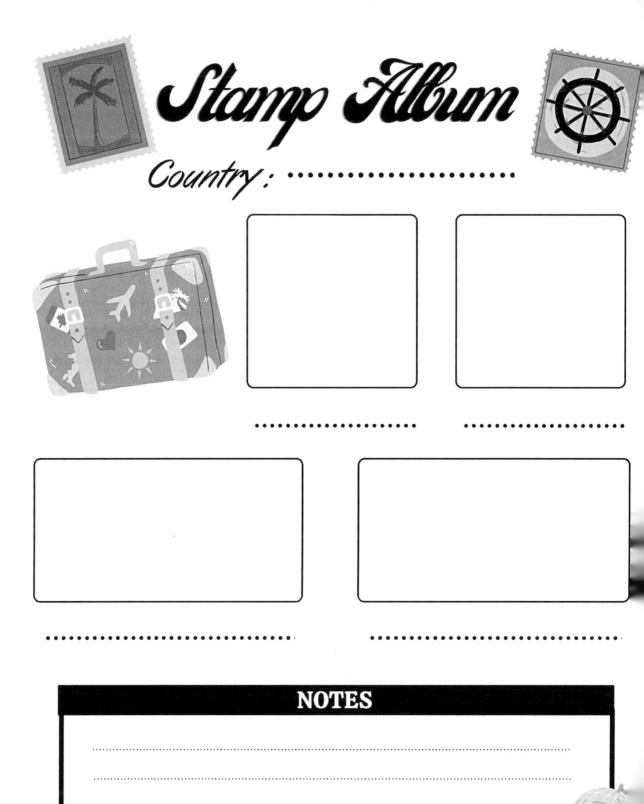

....

....

NOTES

....
....
....
....
....

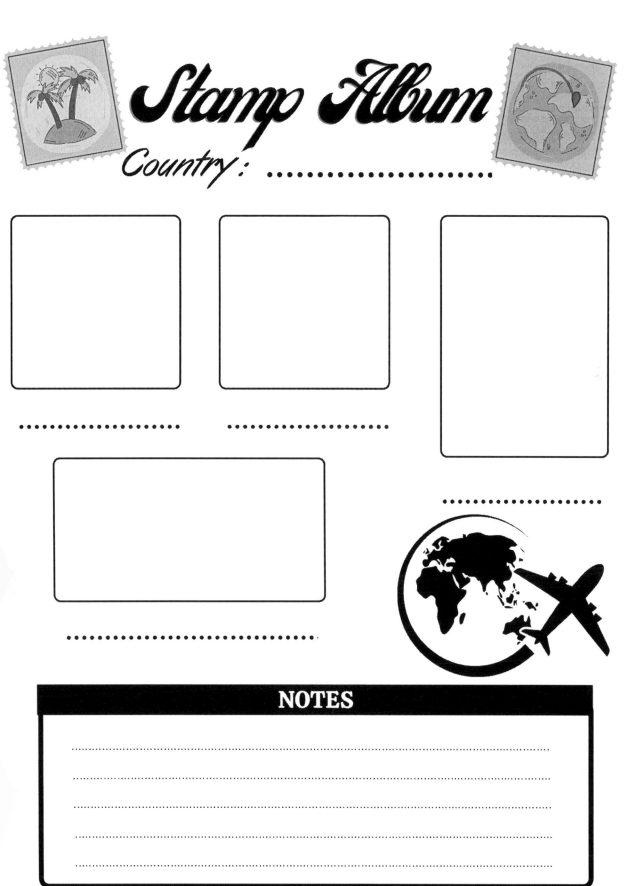

Stamp Album

Country: ....

NOTES

Stamp Album

Country: ....

NOTES

Stamp Album

Country: ....

....

....

....

....

NOTES

....

....

....

....

....

Stamp Album

Country: ....

....

....

....

....

NOTES

Stamp Album

Country: ....

NOTES

....
....
....
....
....

Stamp Album

Country: ....

....

....

NOTES

....

....

....

....

....

Stamp Album

Country: ....

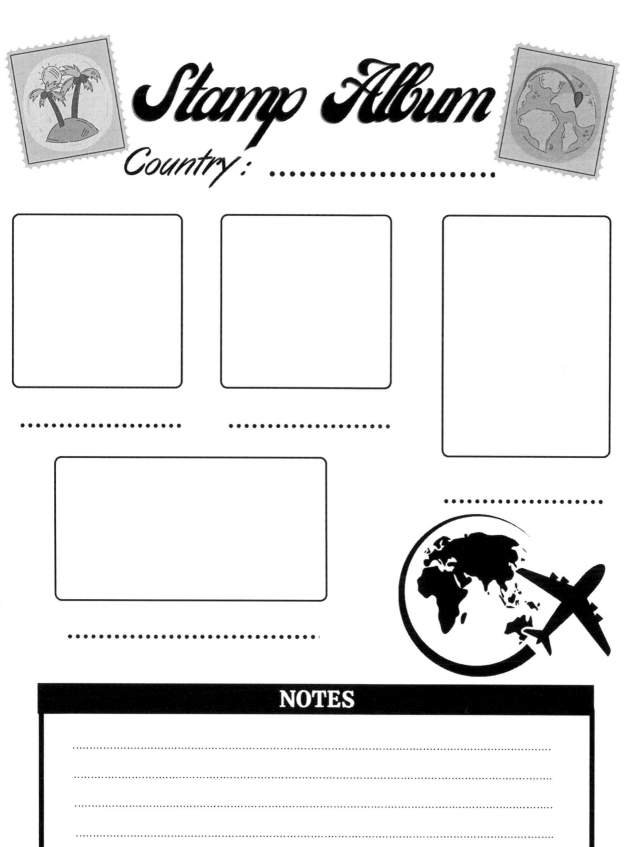

....

....

....

....

NOTES

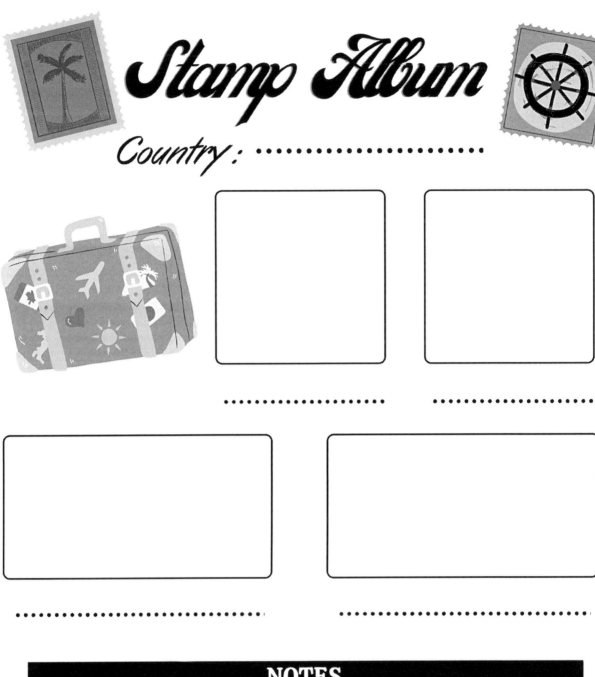

Stamp Album

Country: ....

NOTES

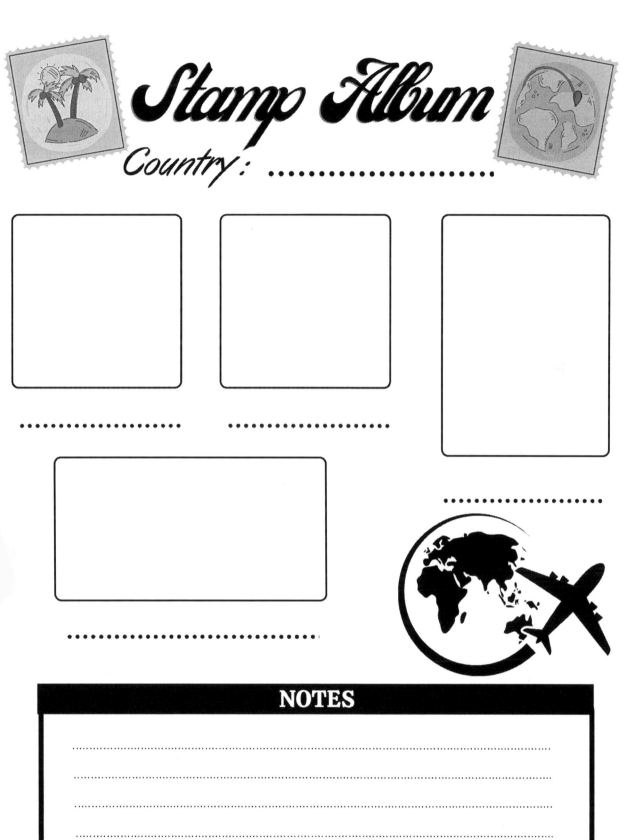

Stamp Album

Country: ....

NOTES

Stamp Album

Country: ....

....

....

NOTES

....
....
....
....
....

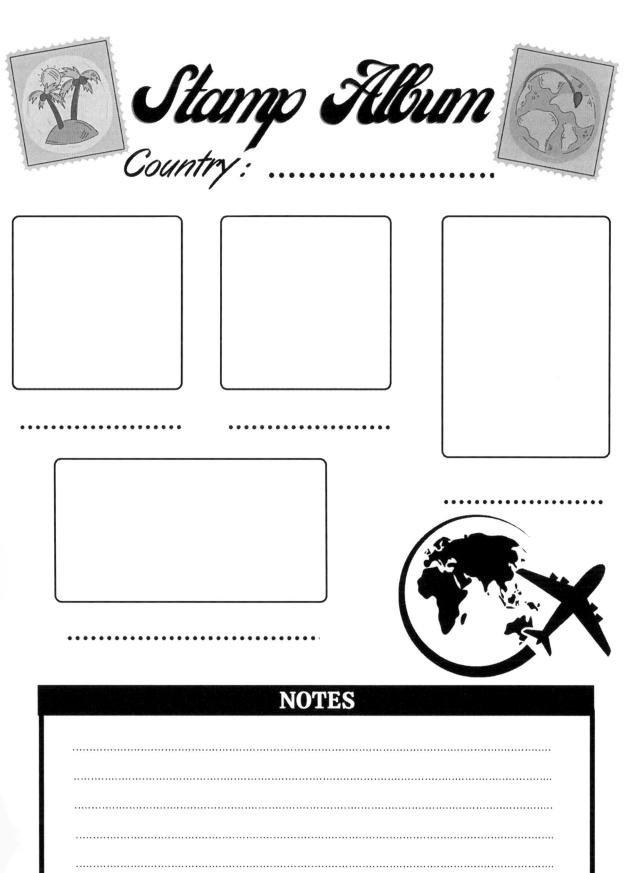

Stamp Album

Country: ....

NOTES

Stamp Album

Country: ....

....

....

NOTES

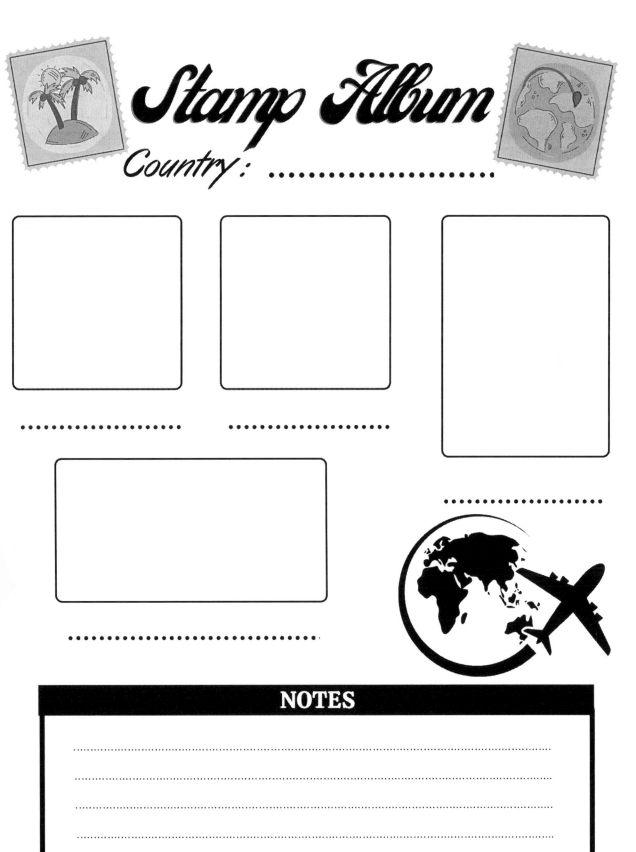

Stamp Album

Country: ....

NOTES

Stamp Album

Country : ....

....

....

NOTES

....

....

....

....

....

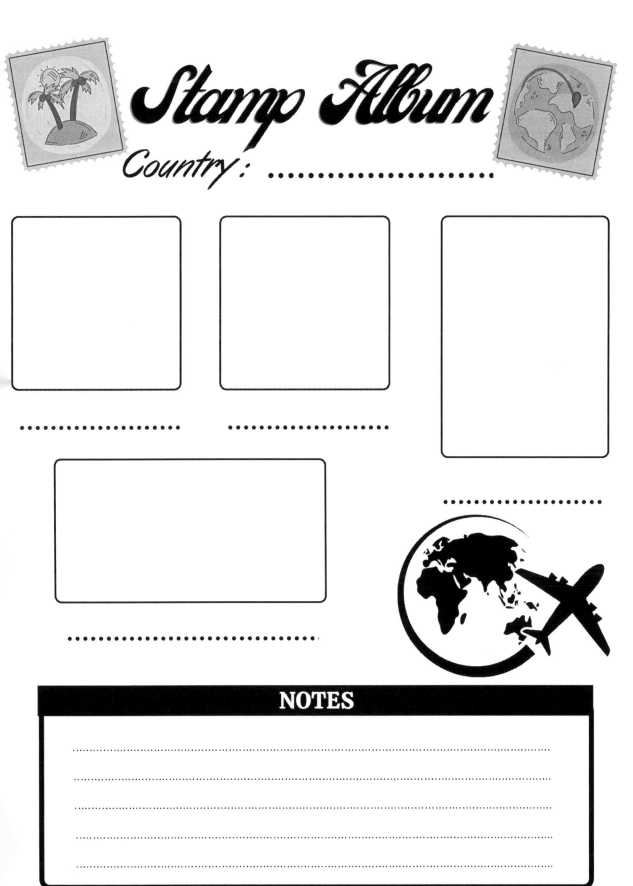

Stamp Album

Country: ....

NOTES

Stamp Album

Country: ....

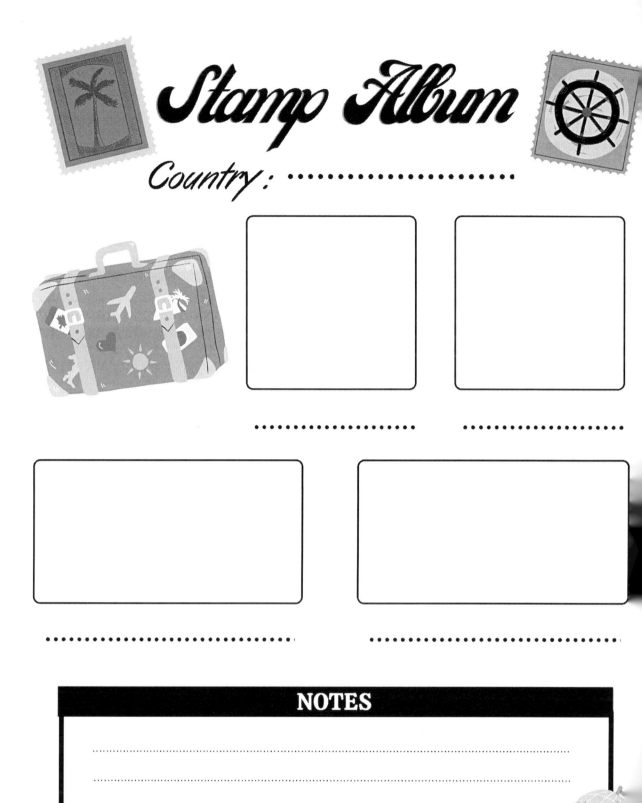

....

....

NOTES

Stamp Album

Country: ....

....

....

....

NOTES

....

....

....

....

....

Stamp Album

Country: ....

....

....

NOTES

....

....

....

....

....

Stamp Album

Country: ....

NOTES

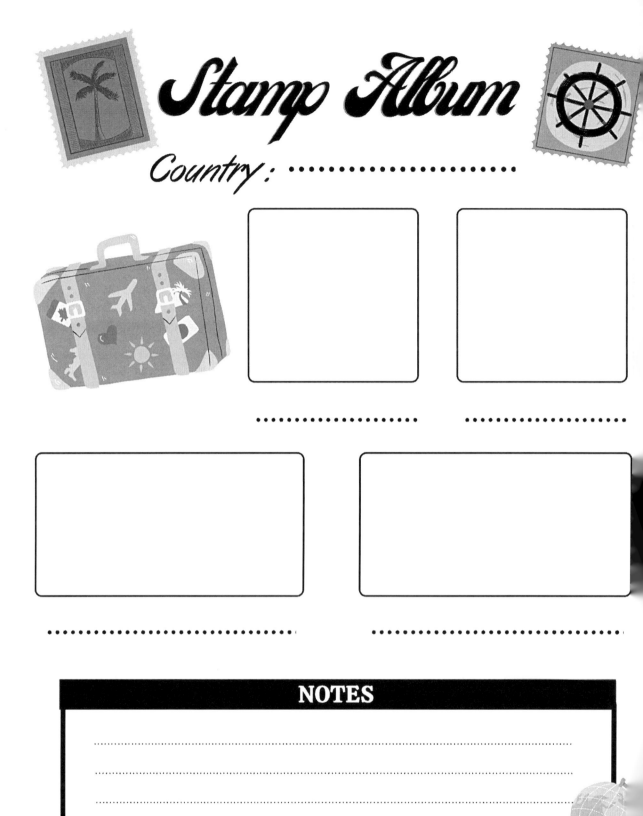

Stamp Album

Country: ⋯⋯⋯⋯⋯⋯⋯⋯

NOTES

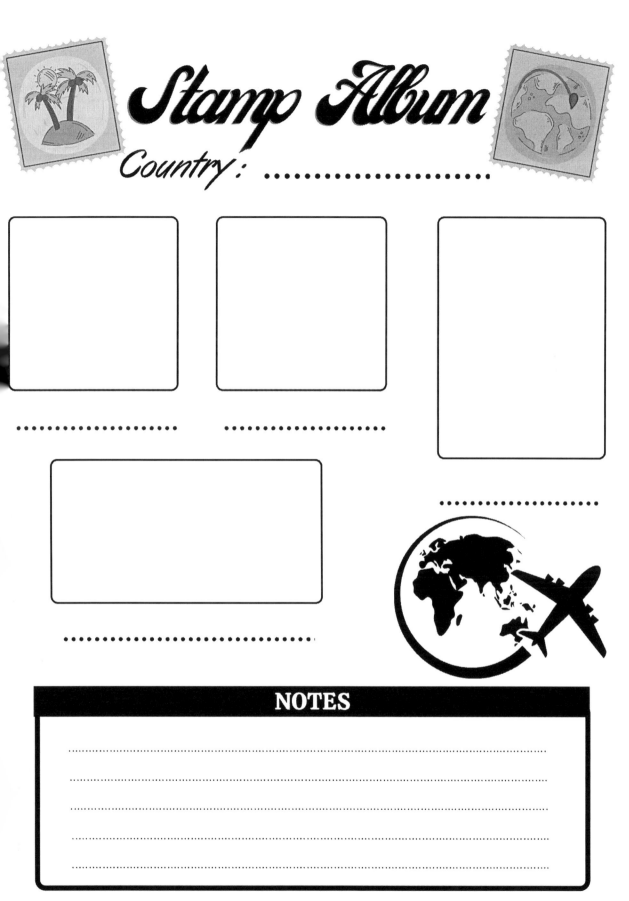

Stamp Album

Country: ....

NOTES

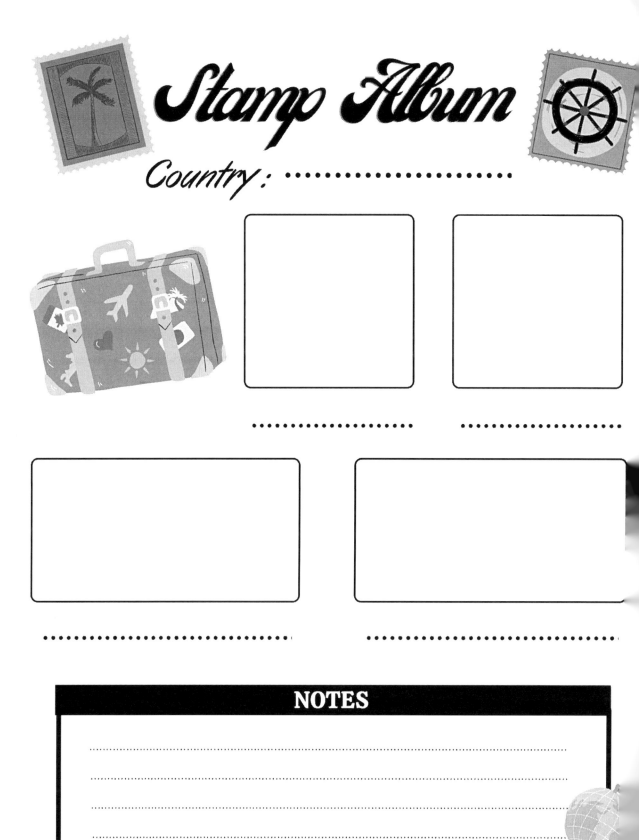

Stamp Album

Country: ....

NOTES

Stamp Album

Country: ....

NOTES

Stamp Album

Country: ....

NOTES

....
....
....
....
....

Stamp Album

Country: ....

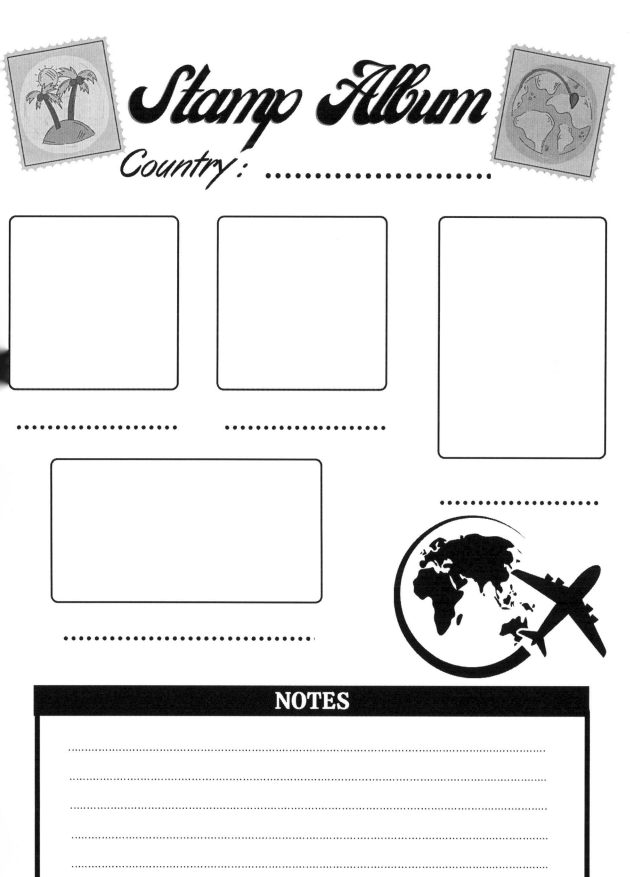

....

....

....

....

NOTES

....

....

....

....

....

Stamp Album

Country: ....

NOTES

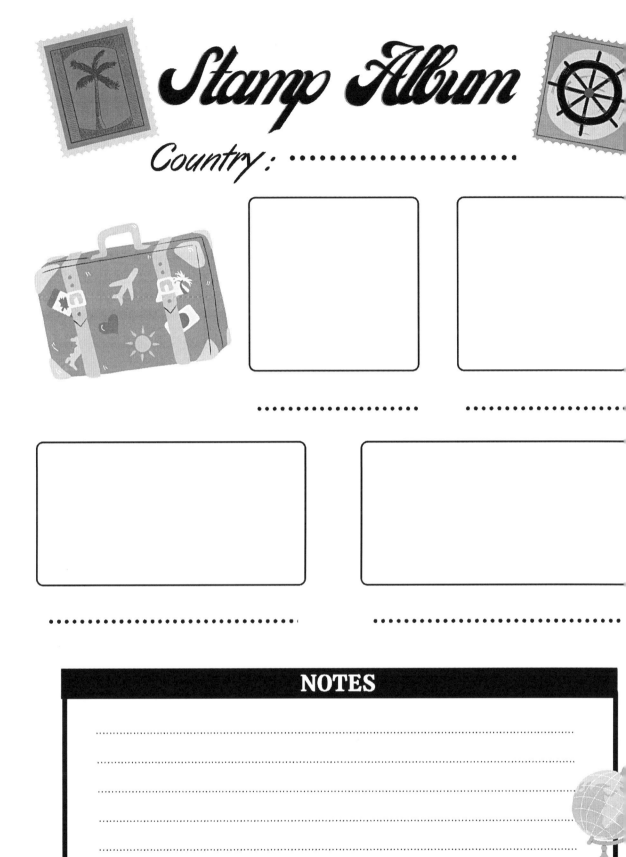

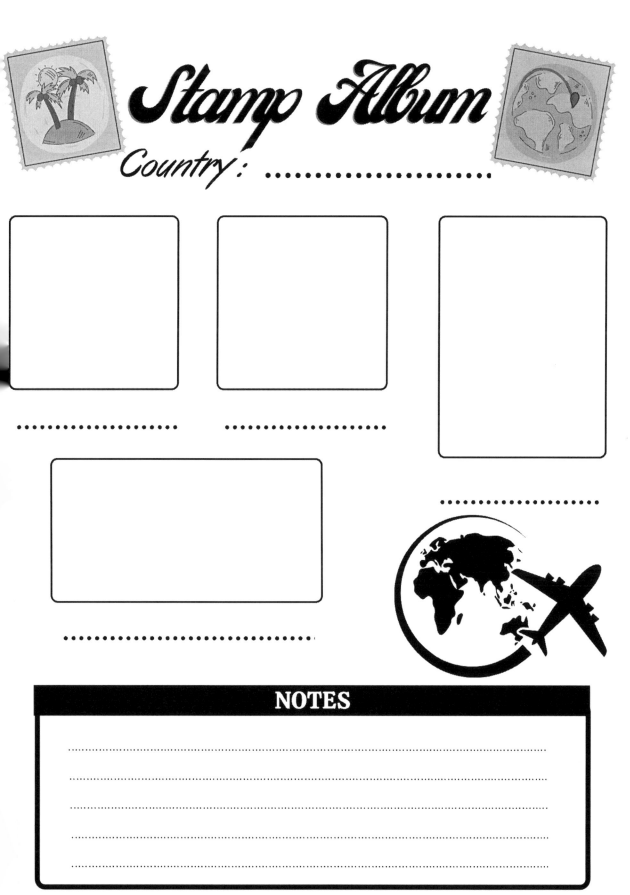

Stamp Album

Country: ....

NOTES

Stamp Album

Country: ....

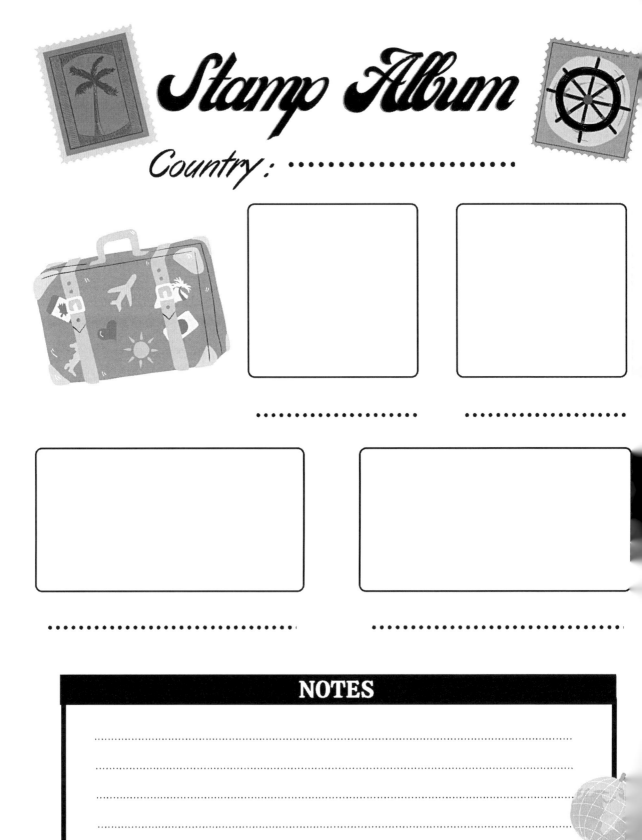

....

....

NOTES

....

....

....

....

....

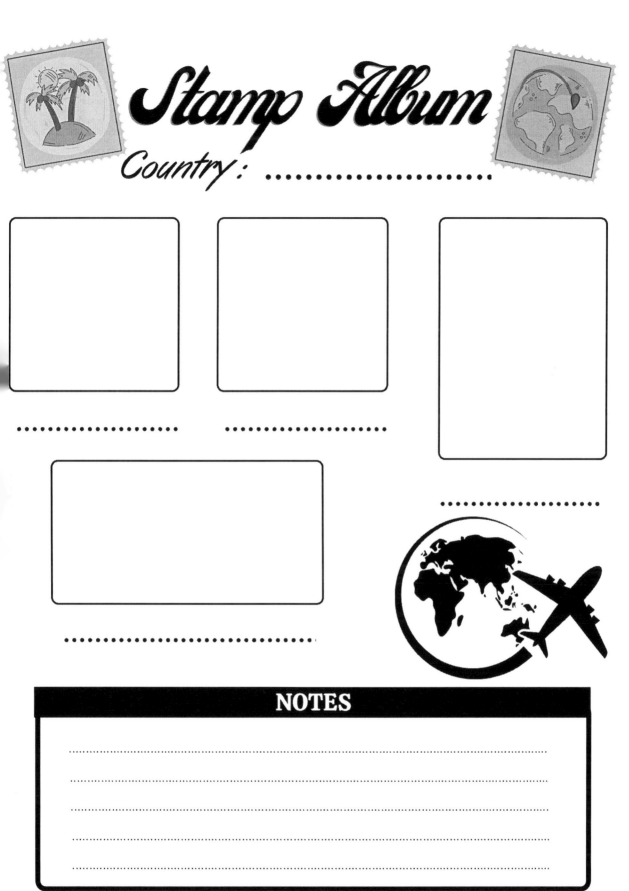

Stamp Album

Country: ....

NOTES

Stamp Album

Country: ....

....

....

NOTES

....

....

....

....

....

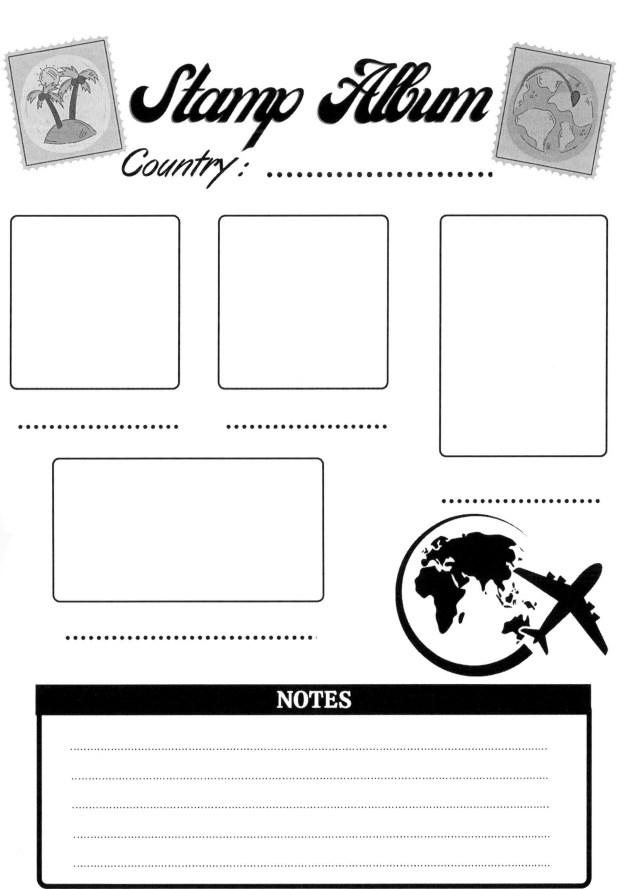

Stamp Album

Country: ....

NOTES

Stamp Album

Country: ....

....

....

NOTES

....

....

....

....

....

Stamp Album

Country: ....

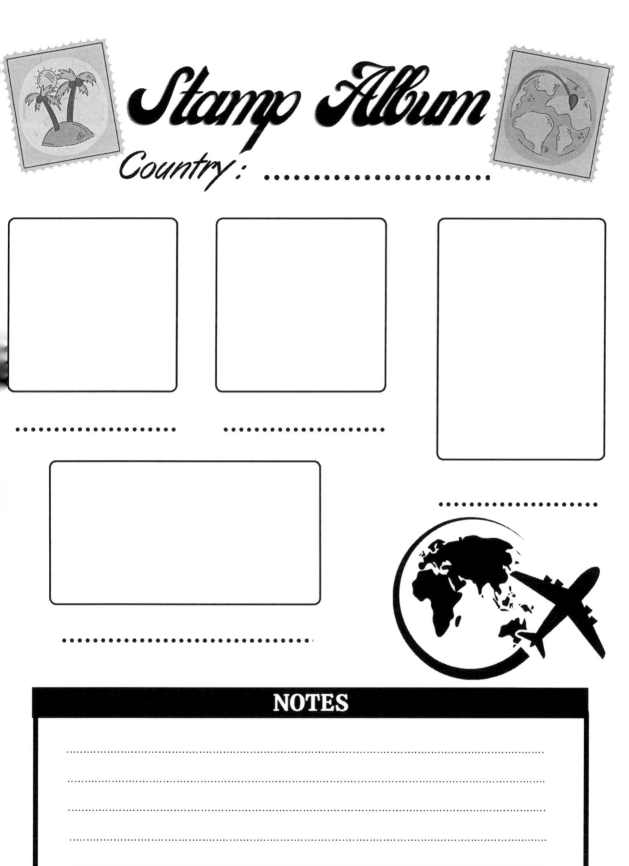

....

....

....

NOTES

....

....

....

....

....

 **Stamp Album**

Country: ....

....

....

NOTES

....
....
....
....
....

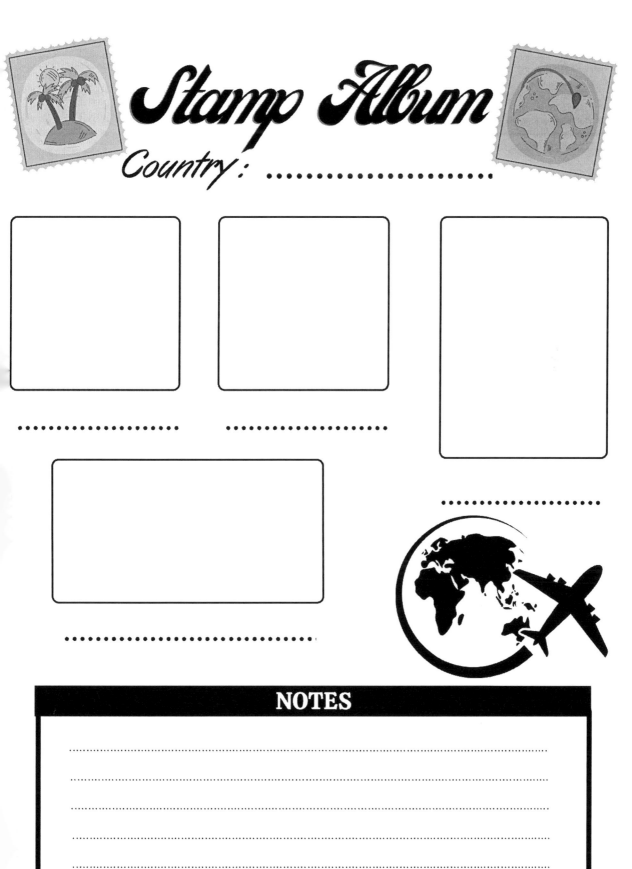

Stamp Album

Country: ....

NOTES

Stamp Album

Country: ·····················

·················· ··················

····························· ·····························

NOTES

···
···
···
···
···

Stamp Album

Country: ....

NOTES

....

....

....

....

....

Stamp Album

Country: ....

....

....

....

....

NOTES

....

....

....

....

....

Stamp Album

Country: ....

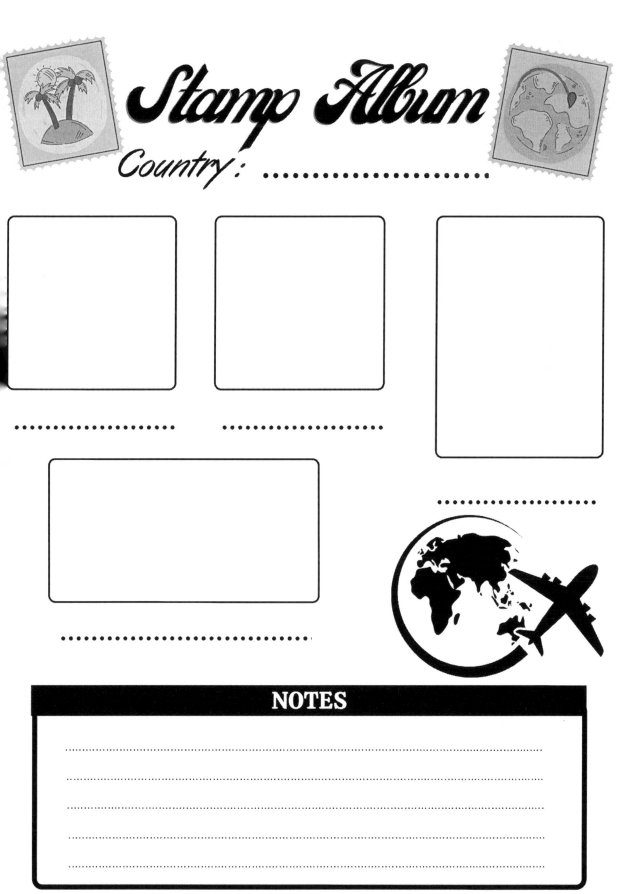

....

....

....

....

NOTES

Stamp Album

Country: ·······················

NOTES

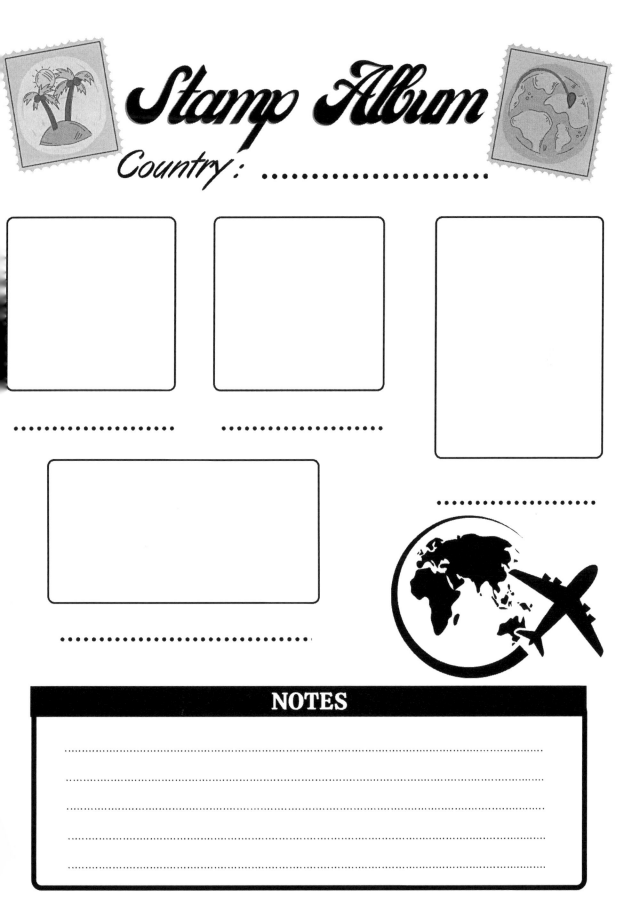

Stamp Album

Country: ....

NOTES

Stamp Album

Country: ·······························

··························· ···························

··························· ···························

NOTES

···
···
···
···
···

Stamp Album

Country: ....

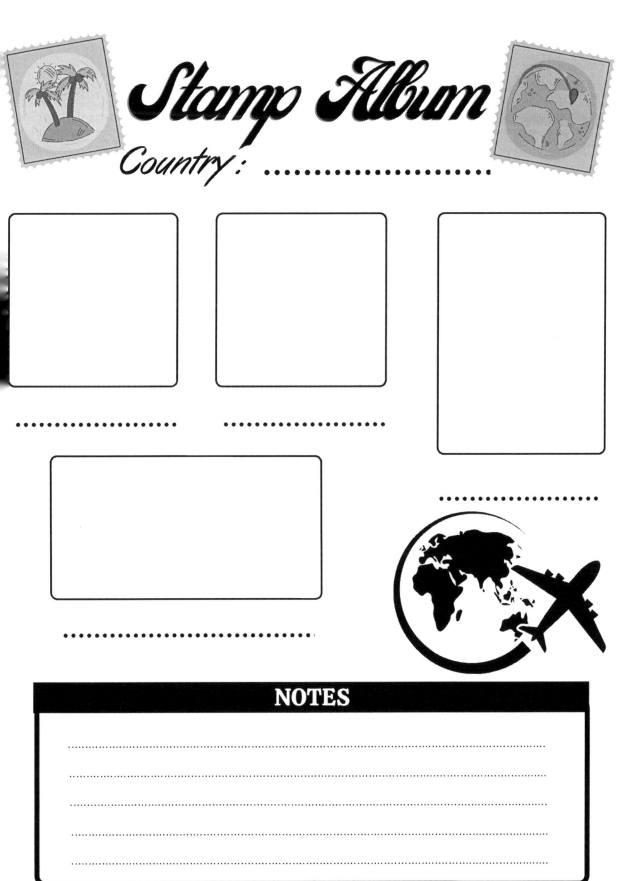

....

....

....

....

NOTES

....

....

....

....

....

Printed in Great Britain
by Amazon

37521831R00070